15 Minutes or Less
Shabbat School
Lessons and Activities

Yahuah Esteem

Why We Say NO to Pagan Christmas

ages 5-14

by
R-Mi Chayil Beyt Yah

TheFightOfLife.com

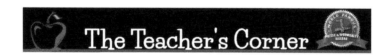

Word Search puzzles were created using the puzzle generators on www.TheTeachersCorner.net.

Puzzles were reprinted in this book with the express written consent of The Teacher's Corner

To Samaya and Samera,

This book was originally created for Samaya More` Johnson and Samera Chavvah Johnson, my two beautiful daughters. It is my hearts' desire to see my children grow in righteousness with a boldness and unashamed love for Yah and His ways. We are destroyed for a lack or knowledge, but in all thy getting get understanding and wisdom is the principle thing. Watching your young, natural curiosity for the word and the things of Yah and seeing you speak up in boldness with a desire for holiness and praise of the Father, nothing has brought me more joy as your mother. The greatest legacy I can leave is children who know who they are in Yah and desire a life that's pleasing to him above ALL else. You both already exude knowledge, wisdom, and understanding well beyond your years- that only comes from the Father Yah and for that I'm grateful. Thank you Father for entrusting me to be the carrier of such beautiful lives. I have given them to you, so they are yours more than they are mine. May I be a good steward of ALL you have given to me (inside and out), having proper heart position to hear you say, "Well Done." And that you are pleased with the life I lived. HalleluYAH. To you Father is all the praise, the honor, the power, and the glory. And to you...I'm thankful.

Instructions for Use

- All scripture in the book is from the Cepher bible.

- In brackets [ ] and *italicized* you will see an explanation you may give to younger children after some more complex matters.

- Repetition is a plus. Especially for younger children. At times when you read them the italicized explanation in brackets, it will serve better for their understanding if you now go back and repeat that portion of scripture or text you just finished explaining to them.

- Please do not skip lessons or some parts may not make sense in later lessons.

Regardless of what lessons we may try to teach our children, YOU are the greatest tool and resource in your arsenal. You are the greatest example of holiness that they will have the privilege of seeing.

~**Proverbs/Mishlei 22:6** Train up a child in the way he should go: and when he is old, he will not depart from it.

Introduction and Encouragement to Parents

This book will explore the TRUTH about Christmas, why it is wicked and pagan, and why we should not participate in any of its practices or celebrations. This book is created for Israelite parents, in a simplified format, providing you with a definitive statement of truth and supporting evidence to back that truth.

These truths should readily, openly, boldly, and unashamedly be passed along to our children, for righteousness' sake. The world in inherently wicked and against the ways of our Father and unfortunately it's unavoidable.

The world's message has entered or is entering into the gateways of our children in one way, shape, form or another, whether we like it or not. On television, no matter how subtle or overt, the ways of the world and their thoughts are being pushed on our children, through the obvious shows themed around certain holidays at certain times of year to the not so obvious ways that even when it's not "holiday season." They (our children) are constantly being promoted to on what's right and wrong and programmed on what they should desire...Hence, where the term television PROGRAMMING comes in. They are telling you exactly what is going on up front, which is often referred to as 'hiding in plain sight' because many still do not take them at their bold word, believe, or even see what's going on.

Okay, but your children may not view television at all. Well, are they in the public and in some cases even private school system. Every year, when these times roll around schools actively indoctrinate our kids with excitement for wickedness from an early age. For example, during thanksgiving they may do certain craft projects, dress up as pilgrims or Indians, or even color such pictures. All while seeing the decorations around the school change to a Thanksgiving theme. Same for Christmas....everything becomes Christmas themed, from plays, to music and chorus recitals, to the attempting of luring our children into this paganism with gifts.

What child does not desire gifts? Why does the satanic Baphomet statue have children around it, as a part of the statue? That's letting you know a major part of their strategy- indoctrinate young. It so ingrained into this wicked culture to where people even feel guilt or like their child is missing out on something if they do not observe Christmas or cannot give them what's seen as a "big" Christmas.

Okay, but like many Israelite families you may homeschool. But doo your kids ever go outside of the house with you during certain times of year? If they do, especially in places like Wal-mart, the themes change to the pagan symbolisms of whatever holiday it is. It can even be visible just riding down the street during these times. It's unavoidable. These things are entering the gateways of your children. So we MUST be just as diligent in countering the message of the world, for righteousness.

Here are some ideas on how you can better counter the worlds' agenda because trust me your kids want THE GIFTS. Randomly celebrate your kids in righteousness, for example, if they had a great week in homeschool, do something nice for them or even let them pick out a gift they would enjoy from time to time. Every other month or so I take my children to the dollar store, big lots, etc. to pick out some things (with my help of course, for the younger). Some children may even enjoy just a day of baking something yummy with you or playing in nature or even learning something new in nature. Our children enjoy new activities and we try to reward them often for progress. Doing this, coupled with teaching them the ways of righteousness and how wicked these pagan days really are...there will come a time, where they no longer enjoy or desire to celebrate these pagan practices like the world.

For example, my 5-year-old was at her grandmother's house one day. Her grandmother, knowing what we believe, was still deciding to try to entice my daughter on these things and make her jealous– by telling my daughter about all of the gifts she would be getting for her other grandbaby this Christmas and how "big" a Christmas he was going to have. Since we no longer celebrated.

My 5-year-old, with boldness in the sweetest and most innocent tone said, "Oh no, Nana you shouldn't be doing that, that's pagan - that's what wicked people do serving after those false gods and stuff." Now, I do NOT prefer she talk about these things to adults unless her mother or father is present, but I also cannot deny the fact that at times Yah has used her, even as an unsuspecting child to bring conviction and revelation to adults where needed. She talked to them about these things and many other things out of love as she does not want them on the bad side of Yah, but she feels like she has talked to them enough and they don't want to listen so she told me that now she has to do what she has been taught to do by the scriptures and "shake the dirt off her feet and move on."

My daughter does not desire to do Christmas and she has developed a good radar. Whenever she is watching tv or looking at anything that she knows is wicked she will call it out herself and turn the channel or turn the tv off altogether and do something else. I have even asked her at times if she wanted to go to certain places or family members houses and her response during certain times was, "Not if they are going to be doing that Christmas stuff." She wants to stay far away from it.

Of course, she's 5 so her "filter" is not yet fully developed, but the boldness of her at that age is beautiful to me...reminds me a lot of myself at her age. Even though I was NOT taught the things I am teaching her and my youngest daughter. I remember when we were in Wal-mart during "Christmas Season" and soon as we walked in she noticed they had the lights, Christmas trees, and air filled life-sized Santa's all around the store. She pointed at Santa and said almost as loudly as she could, as if there was no one around. "There go that wicked Santa! I don't know why they have that thing in here. (sigh) Oh, wicked people. " (shaking her head)

The point is, you don't want your child looking at the words of Yah or you all crazy like you have a "unicorn's" horn growing out of your forehead. You want them to see the ways of the world as such.

Your children are paying attention, even when you don't know that they are. I cannot tell you how many things I've talked to my daughter about or my husband and myself were speaking to each other about, that seemed much over her head or too complicated for her to digest and understand...But oh, she did and DOES. I cannot tell you how many times we have had situations come up later and she's able to understand exactly what's going on based on something we were talking about long ago that I wasn't even 100% sure she was listening, digesting or understanding...but trust me, when it comes to things like this, just put it in there. You ARE making a difference in the life of your children, even when it's not always obvious on the surface.

I pray that this book is a blessing to you!

~ May Yahuah's perfect holy will be done in your life and the life of your family. In the authority of Yahusha's name.

Pushing Yahuah Aside

For The Traditions of Men

Mark 7:7-8
Isaiah 29:13
Matt. 15:7-9
Matt. 26:41

Many "Christians" believe they are celebrating the birth of the True Messiah (Yahusha) who they call Jesus in error. They blindly go along with the traditions of men, mixed with a little bit of the bible and believe it's okay, because they have been lied to by pastors, ministers, and priests. Even Yahusha himself warned us in Mark 7:7-8 "Howbeit IN VAIN DO THEY WORSHIP ME, [*Explanation to Children: Yahusha is saying that the way they serve Yahuah is vain or empty. For example, if you are thirsty and I hand you an empty cup with nothing in it, can you use that? (Listen to whatever the child has to say and give more examples, if necessary). No, you can not use that and that is what Yah is saying too. These people are showing up like empty cups to me and I can't us that.*] teaching for doctrines THE COMMANDMENTS OF MEN. For laying aside the commandment of Yahuah, [*Explanation: So they rather teach and tell people to do the things that man or people came up with and push aside the things that Yah said to do.*] ye HOLD THE TRADITION OF MEN..." [*Explanation: Let's*

Pushing Yahuah Aside

For The Traditions of

Men

break down the word tradition. Tradition is something that people have been doing over and over for so long, like Christmas, that they forgot or don't know where it really even started or comes from; but many times THAT's what they rather hold to, what their family has been doing, over what Yah is telling them to do.]

Again in Matt.15:7-9 "Ye HYPOCRITES [*Explanation:*

This is Yahusha speaking of the people. A hypocrite is a person that says one thing but does another.] well did Yesha'Yahu/ Isaiah prophesy of you [*Explanation: He's saying, boy did Yesha'Yahu/ Isaiah know what he was talking about when he said this about you.*], saying, 'This people draweth nigh unto me with their mouths, and honoreth me with their lips; but THEIR HEART IS FAR FROM ME. But IN VAIN do they WOR-SHIP me, teaching for doctrines the commandments of MEN"

Key Takeaways

When we do things it is important that we know WHY we do them and where they come from and that we only do things that are pleasing to Yahuah. Many people say they love Yah and think they are serving Yah,

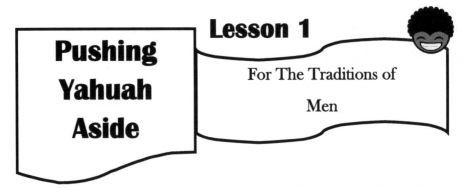

but if they study and take a closer look at scripture [*sidebar: The Hebrew word for scripture is besorah.*] they will see that they are off and shouldn't be doing many of the things that that they do.

Activity

On the next page you will find an activity that will allow for you to practice watching for and seeing things that are not always obvious.

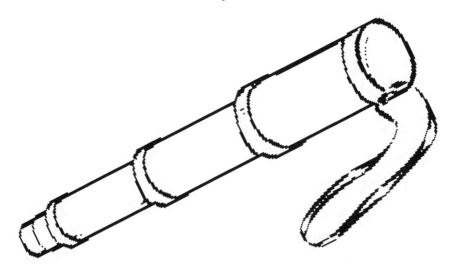

Pushing Yahuah Aside	Lesson 1
	For The Traditions of Men

Find the Hidden Animals

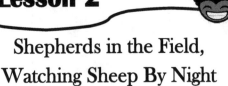

Yahusha's Birth: Part 1

Shepherds in the Field, Watching Sheep By Night

Luke 2:8

Let's Review:

In our last lesson, we learned how it's important to understand why we are doing what we do, especially traditions. We must know where things come from and watch very closely so that we are not fooled into thinking we are doing what's right when we are really doing what's wrong. Some things are hidden from us on purpose, like in the picture example you did to find the hidden creatures. So we have to watch closely to make sure that what we are doing is pleasing to Yah and not in vain.

Now Let's Begin Lesson 2!

Many Christians believe that they are celebrating the birth of the Messiah, but that is false. The Messiah Yahusha (who the world calls Jesus Christ) was born nowhere near December 25th. Yahusha was most likely born in spring, which signifies new birth and when nature comes alive. Spring is also when all of the lambs are born. *Yahusha was also called the

Yahusha's Birth: Part 1

Shepherds in the Field, Watching Sheep By Night

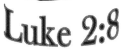

Luke 2:8

sacrificial lamb.

We find that during the time of Yahusha's birth in Luke (Lucas) 2:8 "And there were in the same country shepherds abiding in the field, keeping watch over their flock by night."

We know that when the new baby sheep were born in the spring the shepherds would take turns watching them through the night (3hrs each) to make sure that no beasts of the field, such as wolves, foxes, or other wild animals, ate their flock.

As part of Hebrew custom [*culture, tradition or the Hebrew way*] they would send out their sheep to the desert around Passover or Pesach time, in the spring and bring them home at the beginning of the first rain. The first rain usually happened early in the month of Marcheshvan, which is a Fall/Autumn month that falls on October-November on our calendar. However, the sheep were kept in the open country air or the field all summer. So our Messiah could not have been born past September since the flock was still in the open air/the field at night. No flocks would have been out in the field at all on December

Yahusha's Birth: Part 1

Lesson 2
Shepherds in the Field, Watching Sheep By Night

Luke 2:8

same country shepherds abiding in the field, keeping watch over their flock by night."

And we know that the sheep were born in spring and around Pesach, they would be taken to the desert, where the shepherds would keep watch of them day and night. From this time in spring, all the way through the summer months the sheep were kept in the open air/the field even at night time. So considering this scripture with Hebrew

25th. They would have been brought home on the first rain, at the latest.

Key Takeaways

Luke (Lucas) 2:8 says this was happening when Yahusha was born "And there were in the

customs, it doesn't seem that Yahusha could have been born past September. We can also look at the fact that all sheep would have been brought home in the month of Marcheshvan (October-November) at the latest. So there is no chance that he was born on December 25th. A little later we will talk about whose birth they are really celebrating.

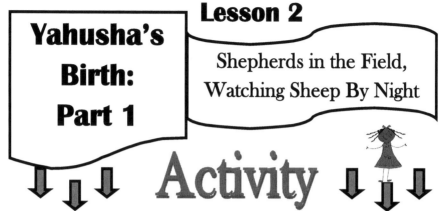

Yahusha's Birth: Part 1

Lesson 2

Shepherds in the Field, Watching Sheep By Night

Activity

Spring has come and the wilderness of Judea is covered in grass for the sheep to eat. Help the shepherd lead his sheep out to the wilderness, where they will be until the first rain, usually in October-November.

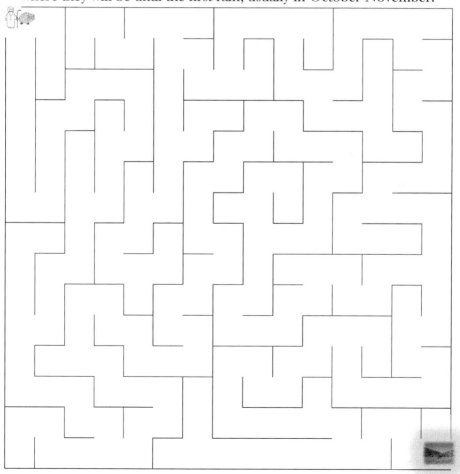

Yahusha's Birth: Part 1

Lesson 2
Shepherds in the Field, Watching Sheep By Night

It is close to the end of September now in Judea. The first rain has not yet come and the sheep are still in the wilderness. Only now the evenings are getting cooler so the sheep will not be left in the open air all night in just a fence, without a more solid shelter to at least block them from any cool winds. It's almost night now. Help the shepherd lead his sheep to the sheepfold.

Yahusha's Birth: Part 2

No Room in The Inn

Luke 2:7
Luke 22:11
Leviticus 23:42-43

There are 4 Holy Days in spring that Yah commanded us to keep to. [*Sidebar: From the word HolyDays they got their word Holidays by changing the y to an i and forming holidays after pagan/wicked/false god worship, that has nothing to do with The Most High's Holy Days.*]

The 4 Holy Days in spring are:

- Passover or Pesach,
- Feast of Unleavened Bread,
- Feast of First Fruits,
- Pentecost (Feast of Weeks) or Shavuot

There are 3 Holy Days in the fall:

- Feast of Trumpets,
- Day of Atonement,
- Feast of Tabernacles or Sukkot

(*This is not a lesson on the Holy Days they are covered in more detail in another book.*)

Some people, who know that the Messiah was not born on Christmas Day, try to say that he must have been born around the fall Holy Day of Sukkot or The Feast of Tabernacles.

Let us look at another scripture

Yahusha's Birth: Part 2

No Room in The Inn

Luke 2:7
Luke 22:11
Leviticus 23:42-43

that talks about the birth of Yahusha:

Luke [*Lucas*] 2:7 "And she [*Mary or Miryam*] brought forth her firstborn son, and wrapped him in swaddling clothes, and laid him in a manger; because there was no room for them in the inn [*malon (hebrew), katalyma (greek)*]."

If Yahusha had been born during the time of the Feast of Tabernacles, they would not have been looking for room in the inn [*malon (hebrew), katalyma (greek)*]. [*Explanation: An inn is like a hotel.*] They would have gone to their family tents and stayed there or built their own. During the Feast of Tabernacles, all the Israelites had to live in booths or tents/sukkahs for seven days to remember how when Yah brought them out of Egypt they had to live in tents/sukkahs. (*Leviticus or Vayiqra 23:42-43*)

So, there would have been plenty of room available in the inn during the Feast of Tabernacles or Sukkot, when all of the Israelites were in tents/sukkahs and Joceph and Miryam (Mary) would not have been looking to stay at the inn [*malon (hebrew)*] either. (continue...)

Luke 2:7
Luke 22:11
Leviticus 23:42-43

Later in life, Yahusha himself sought out an inn, guest room or *malon* during Passover (*Pesach*) to eat with his disciples.

Luke [*Lucas*] 22:11 "and say to the goodman [*owner*] of the house, 'The Master says unto you [*asks*]: Where is the guestchamber [*guest room, malon (Hebrew) katalyma (Greek)*] where I may eat the Passover with my Talmidiym [*disciples*]?'

So given what we see in this lesson, it is very unlikely that Yahusha would have been born on the Fall Holy Day of Sukkot or Feast of Tabernacles.

Four Room House in Israel
No room for Mary up here
Upper room sleeping area
huperoon: "Upper room"
Kataluma: "loosen down"

Open air work court

Mangers and Animal Stables main on floor
Yahusha born here)

www.bible.ca

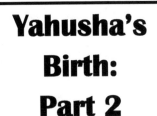

Yahusha's Birth: Part 2

No Room in The Inn

Crossword Puzzle

Use the words below and the clues to help fill in this crossword puzzle.

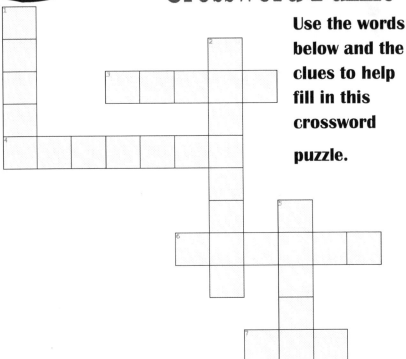

Passover | Lucas | Inn | Tents | Pesach | Sukkahs | Malon

Across

3. Luke in Hebrew is _____.

4. What is the Hebrew word for booths (or tents) where they lived during the Feast of Tabernacles?

6. How do you say Passover in Hebrew? (You may have to review this one with them.)

7. When Yahusha was born, there was no room in the _____.

Down

1. During the time of Sukkot or Feast of Tabernacles what did the Israelites live in?

2. Around what Spring holy day did Yahusha himself look for an inn, guest room or katalyma? Saying, "Where is the guest room, wh

5. What is the Hebrew word for inn or guest room?

Judges 2:12-13

Exodus 31:16-17

Let's Review:

Given our past lessons seeing that the Mary and Joceph were looking for an inn instead of staying at the family sukkah/ tent, make it very unlikely that the Messiah was born on the Fall Holy Day Sukkot. It was during the time of Passover (in spring) when Yahusha himself looked for an inn, guest room [*malon (hebrew), katalyma (greek)*] to eat with his disciples.

And we also saw from the other lesson when we talked about what time of year the Hebrews would have their sheep in the open air country or the field all night - only from spring through summer and then they would take them home altogether at the time of the first rain, which was usually during the month Mar-cheshvan (October-November on our calendar). But it was very unlikely that the sheep would have been left in the open air all night past even September.

So given those scriptures and looking at Hebrew culture and customs, Yahusha the Messiah would not have been born on December 25th. (Christmas Day)

The Pagan-False God

Judges 2:12-13

Exodus 31:16-17

Now Let's Begin Lesson 4!

So that brings up a question: If Yahusha was not born on Christmas Day, who was?

The answer is the pagan false god, Nimrod. Nimrod, also known as Baal, also known and

Tammuz (they believed that after he died he was reincarnated or brought back to life as Tammuz). You can find many scriptures on Nimrod (*Baal*) in the besorah (*scriptures*). Here is one that sounds just like many of the Israelites today,

Judges/Shofetiym 2:12-13 "And they forsook YAHUAH ELOHIYM of their fathers, which brought them out of the land of Mitsrayim (Egypt), and followed other elohiym (gods), of the elo-hiym (*gods*) of the people that were around them, and bowed themselves unto them, and provoked YAHUAH to anger. 13 And they forsook [*turned their backs on*] YAHUAH, and served Baal and Ashtaroth (*which is Ishtar or Easter, Nimrods' mother*)."

Nimrod is also known as the sun-god, which is why Yah's holy day of Shabbat is ignored by most Christians and was changed to Sunday, even though

The Pagan-False God

Lesson 4

Born on Christmas

Judges 2:12-13

Exodus 31:16-17

Yah did not give them permission to do this. They did this to honor Nimrod, the sun-god, worshipping the sun-god on sun-day. Exodus/Shemot 31:16-17 "Wherefore the children of Yisra'el shall guard the Shabbat, to observe the Shabbat throughout their generations, for a perpetual (*ongoing*) covenant (*agreement*). 17 It is a sign between me and the children of Yisra'el forever: for in six days YAHUAH made the heavens and the earth, and on the seventh day he rested, and was refreshed.

Okay, so we already know that Easter is pagan and wicked too. Easter is named after a woman named Ishtar or Easter, who was Nimrods' mother. Remember the Easter eggs you see all the time around Easter? One of the reasons they have an egg for Easter is to show conception [*a baby had been made*] and is expected to be born or "come *from the egg*." A woman carries a baby in her belly for 9 months. So let's count the months from Easter [*Easter can fall anywhere between March 22 and April 25th.*] to Christmas at the end of December. You will see that you come to almost 9mths. Some babies can come late, some can

Judges 2:12-13

Exodus 31:16-17

come early, but you see it's almost 9mths.

So we can see that Easter represents when the pagan false god Nimrod was conceived [*made*], then Christmas is really the celebration of his pagan birth [*when HE was born NOT when the true messiah Yahusha was born*].

It was Rome (*The Roman Catholic Church*) that placed the birthday of Yahusha [*who they call Jesus*] on a day when they were already celebrating the birth of Nimrod, who at this time was referred to as Sol Invictus which means the "unconquered sun" (*Nimrod*), who was the official [*main*] god of the Roman Empire from the year 274 AD.

December 25th was already celebrated [*as the birthday of the sun-god*] for thousands of years before the true Messiah (Yahusha) was even born.

So when people celebrate Christmas, who are they really celebrating?

Lesson 4

The Pagan-False God

Born on Christmas

Word Scramble

Name: _____

1. MDIRNO	When people celebrate Christmas what false god are they really celebrating?
2. LABA	Another name for Nimrod?
3. MUTMAZ	They believe that after Nimrod died he was brought back to life as _____.
4. HAHAUY	Judges/Shofetiym 2:13 says "And they forsook (turned their backs on) _____, and served Baal and Ashtaroth"
5. HRTEMO	Ishtar or Easter is Nimrods' _____.
6. AMED	The holiday Easter is when Nimrod was conceived or _____.
7. BNRO	Christmas is when Nimrod was _____, NOT the true Messiah.
8. IHARBTDY	December 25th was already celebrated, as the _____ of the sun-god, thousands of years before the true Messiah (Yahusha) was even born.
9. HABBSTA	Exodus/Shemot 31:16-17 tells us to guard and observe this thoughout all of our generations, for a perpetual (ongoing) convenant. Saying it is a sign between us and YAHUAH forever: in six days YAHUAH made the heavens and the earth, and on this day he rested.

The Way of the Heathen

The Start of Christmas

Jeremiah 10:1-5

Let's Review:

So who are people really celebrating when they celebrate Christmas? If you remember our last lesson, then you know this answer is Nimrod, Baal, Tammuz, the sun-god. His mother is Istar or Easter, which is where the Easter holiday comes from and it is also the time when Nimrod was conceived or made, sometime between March and April. So if we count forward 9mths we come to around the time of the pagan birth, December 25th. These pagan holidays are connected. Christmas day was already celebrated for thousands of years, as Nimrods' birthday, long before the true Messiah [*Yahusha Ha-Mashiach or Yahusha the Messiah or Anointed One*] was even born. It was Rome who decided to place the birthday of who they call Jesus in error [*Yahusha*] on December 25th, a day when they were already celebrating the birth of Nimrod.

◆◆◆◆◆◆◆◆◆

Now Let's Begin Lesson 5!

Jeremiah/Yirmeyahu 10:1-5 Describes an ancient Christmas cel-

The Way of the Heathen

The Start of Christmas

Jeremiah 10:1-5

ebration ritual that people were doing long before the birth of the true Messiah and much of it will sound similar to how you still see Christmas or sun-god worship being celebrated on Christmas to this day.

Jeremiah/ Yirmeyahu 10:1-5

"HEAR ye the Word which YAHUAH speaks unto you, O house of Yisra'el: 2 Thus says YAHUAH, Learn not the way of the heathen and be not dismayed at them. [*Yah is saying don't do what the wicked people do and don't be shocked by it.*] 3 For the customs of the people are vain: [*So we see this again, Yah is saying that their ways and traditions are vain or empty*] for one cuts a tree out of the forest, the work of the hands of the workman, with the axe. [*He's saying they cut down their trees from the forest, think of a Christmas tree*] 4 They deck it with silver and with gold; they fasten it [*hold it down*] with nails and with hammers, that it move not. [*Think of all the pretty silver and gold decorations people dress their tree up with*] 5 They are upright as the palm tree, but speak not: [*Yah is saying, look how crazy it is for them to chase after these false gods. He says*

Jeremiah 10:1-5

the tree may stand up straight, but it can't speak, not like the one True Elohiym.] they must needs to be borne, because they cannot go. [*He says, the tree even needs to be carried because it cannot walk. (Ask the younger child rather jokingly:*

Have you ever seen a tree walk?)] Be not afraid of them; for they cannot do evil, neither also is it in them to do good. [*He's saying that these dead false gods that they are worshipping after are as powerless as that tree and the tree cannot do bad or good. (Ask the younger child these questions jokingly again and give them time to respond to each one: Have you ever seen a tree fight? Use a bad word? Cook dinner? Or hand* someone a gift to make them smile?*)]

The Way of the Heathen

The Start of Christmas

Jeremiah 10:1-5

The Start of Christmas

The wicked Roman empire would hold a festival every year called Saturnalia. The festival would last for 8 days, going from December 17-25, celebrating their false god Saturn.

It was winter and plants were dying.

They saw Saturn as their god of harvest and agriculture, to help the plants grow. But since it was winter and plants were dying, they thought Saturn needed help at this time. Help, from the sun-god (*dramatic music: doom, doom, doom*).

They believed that human sacrifice or killing children and babies and offering their dead bodies to their false god, would help to strengthen the sun. During the time of this festival the courts were closed and the city was even more lawless than usual, so that no one could get in trouble for what they did during the 8 days of the festival.

The festival would begin by each Roman community choosing a victim. They would bully and abuse this person that whole week and force them into doing things that they didn't want to do

Jeremiah 10:1-5

with their bodies. On the last day of the festival, December 25th, they would murder this innocent man or woman, believing that they were destroying the forces of darkness.

In the 4th century, The Roman Catholic Church now wanted to take this pagan festival to the masses, to more pagan people. So the Catholic leaders got many people to convert or turn to Christianity by promising them that they could still celebrate Saturnalia as "Christmas." And the church agreed to allow the holiday to be celebrated on Christmas the same as it has always been during Saturnalia.

So the earliest Christmas holidays were celebrated with murdering of innocent men, women, and children, drinking, singing naked in the streets (*which is where Christmas Carols come from*), massive orgies and fornication in the streets- where men, women and children did things that Yah said are only supposed to be done by a man with his wife and more. It was a very wild, crazy and wicked time that Yahuah our Elohiym frown upon.

And to make the festival more "Christian", they lied and said

The Way of the Heathen

Lesson 5

The Start of Christmas

Jeremiah 10:1-5

that they will just say that December 25th was the day Jesus was born. But we know, the real Messiah was NOT born December 25th and his name was not Jesus. They changed all of these things to keep people serving pagan false gods

and try to mock or make fun of the one true and living Elohiym Yahuah, by tricking the most precious thing he created into believing a lie.

Many people want to believe that for them Christmas is just a time for joy, love, to be merry and get together with family. That is false. If you are doing anything in celebration because of Christmas then you are bringing these wicked spirits onto yourself and your participating

family.

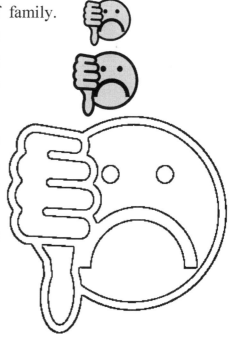

Word Search

Look across and down to find words hidden in the puzzle.

```
H  S  J  O  G  N  U  U  N  V
Y  A  C  E  U  Z  H  O  H  L
A  T  V  X  W  L  O  Z  P  M
H  U  G  W  R  D  L  R  A  T
E  R  K  I  L  L  I  N  G  R
A  N  J  C  V  O  D  P  A  E
T  A  U  K  V  U  A  E  N  E
H  L  Y  E  A  H  Y  L  B  L
E  I  V  D  I  C  Y  I  A  H
N  A  P  U  N  Q  Y  E  L  Y
```

TREE	VAIN
HEATHEN	YAH
SATURNALIA	KILLING
PAGAN	HOLIDAY
LIE	WICKED

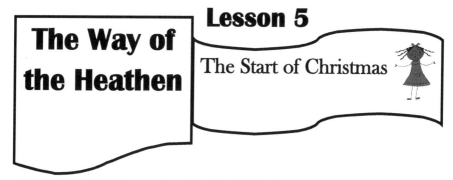

Lesson 5

The Way of the Heathen

The Start of Christmas

Help the Hebrew family find their way out of the pagan maze.

YOU DID IT!

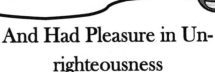

Lesson 6

They Believed A Lie

And Had Pleasure in Unrighteousness

2 Thessalonians 2:10-13

1 Peter 5:8

2 Corinthians 11:4

Let's Review:

In Jeremiah 10, we are given a warning not to follow the ways of wicked men. Then it gave us a clue to some of the things these wicked men would be doing and it clearly described how we see people celebrating Christmas today, right? We saw that Christmas started with the pagan Saturnalia festival. The festival filled with bullying, murdering/killing innocent men, women, and children, doing things against Yah that He does not want us to do with our bodies, and more. This was a very evil festival, but Rome wanted to take it to more people.

So they lied and said that December 25th was the day the Messiah (*HaMashiach*) was born and they got many pagan people to join Christianity by promising them that they could still do their dirty Saturnalia festival only now as Christmas.

Many people want to believe that for them Christmas is just a time for joy, love, to be merry, and get together with family. That is false. If you are doing anything in celebration because it's Christmas season then you are bringing these wicked spirits onto yourself and your partici-

Lesson 6

They Believed A Lie

And Had Pleasure in Unrighteousness

2 Thessalonians 2:10-12

1 Peter 5:8

2 Corinthians 11:4

pating family.

Now Let's Begin Lesson 6!

2 Thessalonians/*Tasloniqiym* 2:10-12 10And with all deceivableness of unrighteousness in them that perish [*Explanation: They believed a lie and that caused them to do things that went against Yah and so they were destroyed.*];

because they received not the love of the truth, that they might be saved [*They didn't love the truth enough, they had some things that they still wanted to hold on to. They wanted that more than they wanted the hard truth and the truth can be hard sometimes, but we take it and love it because it's good for us. Like if you have a cold, some- times you have to take medicine or things that do not taste so well, but you do it and it helps you to feel better. It's like that! Some people hate the taste of some truths so much that they rather stay sick, than get well. So like this scripture says, they couldn't be saved or helped.*]

11And for this cause God shall send them strong delusion, that they should believe a lie: 12That they all might be damned who believed not the truth, but had

They Believed A Lie

And Had Pleasure in Unrighteousness

2 Thessalonians 2:10-13

1 Peter 5:8

2 Corinthians 11:4

pleasure in unrighteousness. [*So Yah allowed these wicked men to send out these lies, to show who REALLY has a love for the truth and who doesn't. Because if someone has a love for the truth, they will eventually find their way out of the* lies.]

1 Peter/*Kepha* 5:8   8Be sober, [*Explanation: Pay attention*] be vigilant [*Watch closely*]; because your adversary [*An adversary is someone who is against you, someone who wants you to fail or not do well*] the devil, as a roaring lion, walketh about, seeking whom he may devour [*or eat up*]

2 Corinthians/*Qorintiym* 11:4 For if he that comes preaches another Yahusha [*savior, salvation*], whom we have not preached [*if someone else comes along and try to show you another way or give you a different elohim*], or if you receive another ruach [*spirit*], which you have not received [*or if you get involved with things that cause you to take on evil spirits, not of Yah*], or another Besorah [*scripture*], which you have not accepted, you might well bear with him [*This might cause it to*

They Believed A Lie

And Had Pleasure in Unrighteousness

2 Thessalonians 2:10-12

1 Peter 5:8

2 Corinthians 11:4

stay and be harder to get rid of and that's exactly what we see has happened today with Christmas. If we allow wrongdoing with ourselves, it will be harder to get rid of later.]

Let's Go into Some Christmas Symbols and What They Actually Mean:

The Christmas Tree:

Nimrod's mother Ishtar/Easter told people this story. She said, that when Tammuz (aka Nimrod) was killed, some of his blood dripped onto an evergreen tree and the tree grew into a full grown new tree overnight. This made the evergreen tree special to them, by the blood of their false god Tammuz.

Also, since the Christmas tree does not seem to die and stays green all winter. The evergreen tree was the perfect symbol to show how Nimrod (the unconquered sun) had never really died but had come to life again

They Believed A Lie

And Had Pleasure in Unrighteousness

as Tammuz.

2 Thessalonians 2:10-13

1 Peter 5:8

2 Corinthians 11:4

Santa Claus:

Let's look at the spelling of the name Santa very closely. [*Remember we must watch very closely.*] S-A-N-T-A. Now, let's look at the word Satan. S-A-T-A-N. [*For younger children, they may need more assistance to see this. So, every time you call out a letter to spell S-A-T-A-N, have them put a slash through that letter on Santa. This will help them see it for themselves in a hands-on manner.*]

As you can see, Santa and Satan have the same letters. Some of the letters have just been switched around. This is called an anagram. This is one way that wicked people may try to hide things. So that you won't know what's going on.

But they are telling you, in plain sight, we just had to look a little closer to see it- what spirit is behind the character Santa. Satan is against Yah our Elohym. It is him that is behind every wicked

They Believed A Lie

Lesson 6

And Had Pleasure in Unrighteousness

2 Thessalonians 2:10-13

1 Peter 5:8

2 Corinthians 11:4

thing you see that goes against Yah. Satan loves to copy Yah and always tries to be like him in every way. So that's why Santa comes off like an all-knowing false god. Think about it, he knows when you're sleeping and knows when you're awake? That's like saying he's everywhere, at everyone's house all at once. That's called omnipresent. Only Yah is omnipresent - everywhere at the same time and only Yah is all knowing, knows everything. Satan is a fake and an imposter who loves to trick Yah's people.

The other part of Santa's name, Clause, was made to spookily sound close to claws. You know, like animal claws. So let's put it together in truth, Santa Claus equals Satan's Claws [*for younger children make hand motions like claws*] and no one should get caught up in Satan's Claws.

Santa is also a mixture of a lot of false gods put together into one, to form Santa Claus. All of the false gods that make up the "special powers" of Santa can be traced back to Nimrod. Yes, Nimrod has everything to do with Christmas.

They Believed A Lie

And Had Pleasure in Unrighteousness

2 Thessalonians 2:10-13

1 Peter 5:8

2 Corinthians 11:4

Have you ever heard Santa called St. Nick or St. Nicholas. Nicholas means "mighty one, powerful."

Here are some of the false gods Santa is mixed with:

- It was the pagan god Odin who left gifts during the

"Yuletide" season, under an evergreen tree, which was his special tree. Odin, Adon, Adonis, or Nimrod were the same. They both were the great "war-god." Nimrod (*as Bacchus*) was the "god of wine." Odin ate/drank no other food but wine. Odin has a son named Balder or Baalzer and Baalzer is also known as the son of Baal or Nimrod. (The Two Babylons, p. 133-134)

- **Santa's Helper's (Elves)** Are his slaves, workers or demons. From Olde Religion, his main helper was called the Dark Helper and he was a slave that Santa got from the false god Odin/Nimrod. The Dark Helper

They Believed A Lie

And Had Pleasure in Unrighteousness

2 Thessalonians 2:10-12

1 Peter 5:8

2 Corinthians 11:4

was nonother than Satan, The Dark One, The worker of evil. Of course Santa, the fat jolly old elf, is an elf himself as well. [*The Dark Helper was also called Herne/Pan. This dark helper goes by many different names in different places.*]

- Santa's a mixture of the false goddess Hertha. It was her who they believed entered the house through the chimney, appeared in the fireplace, and brought "good luck tidings" to the home. (Worldbook Encyclopedia)
- Both Norse pagan gods Thor and Tomte were said to ride across the sky in chariots, pulled by goats and gave children gifts at the end of the year.

And more!

Santa is just Satan in disguise and one big jolly mixture of a lot of pagan gods, put together.

The Reindeer:
Remember how Santa is mixed

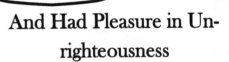

2 Thessalonians 2:10-12

1 Peter 5:8

2 Corinthians 11:4

with the false gods Thor and Tomte, who were said to ride across the sky in chariots, pulled by goats and gave children gifts at the end of the year? Santa's reindeer represent those goats. A goat, because of it's sometimes rebellious and stubborn nature, has

been used as a symbol of Satan. Like the Baphomet statue (*a goat head on a man's body*) used by Satan worshippers. The goat represents the rebellious one, Satan himself.

The Yule Log:
Represented the dead body of Nimrod. It is burned before Christmas day because they believe he was reborn and never died. So the evergreen Christmas tree represents him coming to life again or being "born-again." In north Europe, the Yule log was burned to honor the pagan god Thor. Their wicked festival would go on until the log burned out, which could take up to 12 days. That's where songs like, "The 12 Days of Christmas" come from.

They Believed A Lie

And Had Pleasure in Unrighteousness

2 Thessalonians 2:10-12
1 Peter 5:8
2 Corinthians 11:4

Christmas Carols:

This started from the Saturnalia festival, when they would get drunk and sing in the streets and do other dirty deeds.

Kissing Under the Mistletoe:

This was to represent and play out all of the lustful, dirty, immoral things they did with each other during the Saturnalia festival (*Explained earlier*).

Christmas Lights:

The lights represent the the birth of the new god (sun-god, Nim-

They Believed A Lie

And Had Pleasure in Unrighteousness

2 Thessalonians 2:10-12

1 Peter 5:8

2 Corinthians 11:4

rod) and the return of the light or sun on the shortest day of the year. The lights on a Christmas tree carries over from when pagans would light candles and fires to try to lure or call back the weakening sun. Candles in the window also let people know that you were participating in the wicked Saturnalia festival.

Christmas Colors (Red,

Green, White, and black...mostly):

Remember Nimrod's connection to the evergreen tree and yule log? These colors are the pagan woodsman colors. See the connection? Woods-man. Also, the pagan god named Holly King, who was represented by a holly plant and an evergreen has these colors attached to his image.

They Believed A Lie

And Had Pleasure in Unrighteousness

2 Thessalonians 2:10-12

1 Peter 5:8

2 Corinthians 11:4

Decking the Halls with boughs of Holly :

This is a popular Christmas song about decorating your home with the holly plant. The false god named Holly King was represented by the holly plant and the evergreen tree.

Wreaths:

These represented the Birth-Death-and Rebirth of Nimrod. Circles have no ends so it is believed to be on-going.

They Believed A Lie

And Had Pleasure in Un-righteousness

2 Thessalonians 2:10-13

1 Peter 5:8

2 Corinthians 11:4

Christmas Tree Balls:

[*May not be appropriate for small children*] These represent "sun-balls" or Nimrod's/ Tammuz balls/ testicles.

And more!

We could go on and on with these symbols, but you see clearly now. Christmas and everything about it is wicked to its' core. It is only a mixture of pagan practices and false gods from many different cultures, all

tying into Baal or Nimrod.

Activity

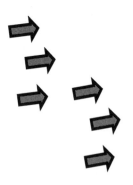

Draw A Line to the Correct Match for Each Problem.

1) pleasure

2) Christmas Tree

3) Santa

4) Elves

5) Reindeer

A) Since this never seems to die, it was chosen as a symbol to show how Nimrod (known as the unconquered sun) had never really died but had come to life again as Tammuz.

B) 2 Thessalonians 2:12 That they all might be damned who believed not the truth, but had _____ in unrighteousness.

C) Like with Thor and Tomte, this animal represents goats pulling Santa in a chariot across the sky. The goat has been used by people who worship Satan as a symbol of the rebellious one, Satan himself.

D) These are Santa's helpers, but they really are a symbol for his slaves, and Satans' evil workers of darkness.

E) Is a mixture of many false gods put together. This is also an anagram- has all of the same letters as SATAN.

Draw A Line to the Correct Match for Each Problem.

6) The Yule Log

7) Christmas Carols

8) Christmas Lights

9) Holly

5) Wreath

F) These represent the return of the sun on the shortest day of the year. These also carry over from when pagans would light candles and fires to try to lure or call back the weakening sun.

G) This started from the Saturnalia festival, when they would get drunk and sing in the streets and do other dirty deeds.

H) This represents the dead body of Nimrod. It is burned before the Christmas tree is put up because they believe he was reborn as Tammuz and never really died.

I) Circles have no ends. So these are used to represent what they believe is the ongoing Birth-Death-and Rebirth of Nimrod.

J) There is a popular Christmas song about decorating your home with this plant. There is also a false god named Holly King who was represented by this plant and an evergreen tree.

Congratulations

Names:_____   _____

_____   _____

_____   _____

_____   _____

_____   _____

YOU HAVE SUCCESSFULLY TAKEN MORE STEPS THAT ARE PLEASING TO YAH, TOWARDS THE LIFE OF HOLINESS HE DESIRES FOR YOU. HALLELUYAH!

Some Notable Research Resources:

Youtube Channels:

Shem Homeschool Academy (video: HOMESCHOOLING PARENTS EDITION: THE TRUE MEANING OF CHRISTMAS!!!!)

Judiyah32 (video: Pagan Holidays - Easter, Christmas & Lent ~ Part 1 and Pagan Holidays - Easter, Christmas & Lent ~ Part 2)

Books & Websites

Worldbook Encyclopedia

The Two Babylons

http://mystery-babylon.org/christmas.html

http://christianitybeliefs.org/the-falling-away/the-names-of-the-father-and-the-son/

http://www.hope-of-israel.org/whenwa~1.htm

http://www.yhrim.com/Teaching_Documents/Yahushas_Earthly_Birth_Month_~_2-5996_-_may_2014.pdf

https://en.wikipedia.org/wiki/Cheshvan

http://biblehub.com/niv/luke/2-8.htm

http://www.hope-of-israel.org/cmas1.htm

https://thetruthandlight.wordpress.com/2008/12/25/saturnalia-the-real-roots-of-christmas/

http://www.paganspath.com/magik/yule-history2.htm

http://www.jerusalem-insiders-guide.com/weather-in-jerusalem.html

http://www.baptistbiblebelievers.com/LinkClick.aspx?fileticket=qDQAYzDf0WM%3D

https://www.worldweatheronline.com/jericho-weather-averages/ps.aspx

Made in the USA
Middletown, DE
12 November 2023

42536651R00033